Finding M: The Great Alphabet Hunt

Paula Curtis Taylorson

illustrated by Anna Semenova

Finding M : The Great Alphabet Hunt

This is a work of fiction.

Text and Illustrations copyrighted

by Paula Curtis Taylorson ©2021

Library of Congress Control Number: 2021904820

All rights reserved. No part of this book may be

reproduced, transmitted, or stored in an information retrieval

system in any form or by any means,

graphic, electronic, or mechanical without prior written

permission from the author.

Printed in the United States of America

A 2 Z Press LLC

PO Box 582

Deleon Springs, FL 32130

bestlittleonlinebookstore.com

sizemore3630@aol.com

440-241-3126

ISBN: 978-1-954191-14-3

Dedication

Thank you to those who read to me and those who listened to me read.

This book belongs to :

_____

Early one **May Monday morning**,
In **Mr Mallory's** old **music** store,
A family of **mice** called the **Murids**,
Mischievously march out their door.

There's **Michelle**, **Morris**, and **Milo**,
Mackenzie, **Mia**, and **Mick**,

Their **momma** and papa are **Macy** and **Max**,
And their grandparents are **Mabel** and **Rick**.

They all **memorise** their **majors** and **minors**,

And they search **manuscripts** covered in song,

Help them discover the **Ms** in the **music** shop,

And keep in **mind** where the **M** words belong!

Each **mouse** is a **miniature musician,**

They play instruments **made** for their size,

Each one is a **marvellous maestro**,

A **micro minstrel** that's full of surprise!

Mr Mallory the manatee manages the shop,
As Mozart the macaw minds the money,

A **meercat** called **Malcolm** comes in every day,
To deliver fresh **muesli** and honey!

A **monkey** who is dressed like a **magician**,

Gives out **marshmallows** and **mints** for a treat,

And **Manuel** the **mailman** wears **mittens** on all of his feet!

Miss Morgan the violin **mistress**,
Speaks **mandarin** to a **muskrat** who
strums a guitar,

And a **Manx** cat stands in front of a **mirror** and sings, '**My**, what a **magnificent** puddy-cat you are!'

A **mallard** is asleep on a **mattress**,

While a **Mexican mariachi** band plays,

And a **mellow moose** who is wearing **mascara**, Squirts a **meddlesome mongoose** with **mild mayonnaise!**

Mabel and Rick dance the **merengue**,
As a **mule** with **maracas** keeps time,

And on the piano a **magpie** is **muttering** to himself,
While **magenta mosquitoes** are flying in line.

Morris thinks **many marine mussels** are hiding,

So **Michelle,** who **mainly** plays the flute,
Blows into the **mouthpiece** of the tuba,

And out of the end the **mussels** all shoot!

Ms Marigold came to buy a new **mandolin**,
She's a beautiful **majestic mermaid**,

She's **married** to a **mammoth** called **Mojo**,
Who **monstrously moved** to the **melody** she played!

This is where **Murids** the **mice** can be seen and be heard,
In **Mr Mallory's** old **music** store,

This time we **mixed** with he **middle** letter **M**, BUT...

There is always room for **many more!**

The End

My Very Own 'M' Words:

Glossary

Page 1. **May** : a month of the year
Monday : a day of the week
Morning : the first part of the day
Mr. : a formal way to address a man
Mallory : a formal name, proper name
Music : the art of sound, combining sounds to make pleasant melodies for enjoyment
Mice : the pleural - more than one - of mouse : a small furry rodent, mammal
Murids : the scientific way to refer to the family classification of mice
Mischievously : playfully annoying, teasing
March : to walk in a regular and measure manner, a beat, deliberate walk
Also on Page 1 : **Mirror** : a reflective Surface to see oneself or copy an image
Musical instruments : objects to make music

Page 2. **Michelle** : a girl's name
Morris : a boy's name
Milo : a boy's name
McKenzie : a girl's name
Mia : a girl's name
Mick : a boy's name

Page 3. **Momma** : a soft or tender name for a mother
Macy : a girl's name
Max : a boy's name
Mabel : a girl's name

Page 4. **Memorize** : to learn something and be able to repeat the facts, impressions, or events without reading or studying them, recalling past events
Majors : in music - it is part of the way music is presented or played - major scales are the greater scales or cords
Minors : in music - it is part of the way music is presented or played - minor scales are the lesser or muted scales or cords
Also on Page 4 : **Menorah** : a Jewish candle

Page 5. **Manuscripts** : music in written form

Page 6. **M** : a letter
Also on page 6 : **Map** : a printed paper with locations of places and monuments
Mushrooms : food

Page 7. **Mind** : (here) watch over
Also on page 7 : **Mask** : something to cover a face, disguise
Milk : food
Mug : a dish to drink from
Marimba : a musical instrument

Page 8. **Mouse** : a small furry rodent, mammal
Miniature : very small,
Musician : someone who plays, Performs or writes music
Also on Page 8 : **Mural** : art on a wall
Magazine :
Magnet :
Money :
Maracas :

Page 9. **Made** : to bring into existence by creating or combining parts Also on Page 9: **Muffins** : food
Mango : food
Market :

Page 10. **Marvellous** : superb, excellent
Maestro : one who conducts, creates, or teaches music

Page 11. **Micro** : very tiny
Minstrel : a musician, singer, or poet, one who sings with a stringed instrument

Page 12. **Manatee** : a sea cow
Manages : to take charge of, to handle, direct, or control an action or use
Mozart : a classical music composer
MaCaw : a colorful bird
Minds : in this book, watches the store and takes care of things that need taken care of
Money : something of worth to exchange for goods- paper money or coins or gold or silver

Page 13. **Meercat** :
Malcolm : boy or man's name
Music : the art of sound - combining sounds to make pleasant melodies for enjoyment

Page 14. **Monkey** :
Magician : an entertainer who practices the art of making something seem like something else

Page 15. **Marshmallows** : sweet food
Mints : food, candy

Page 16. **Moths** : winged insect like a butterfly
Majestically : grand, stately, important
Metronome : a device to keep the pace or rhythm of music

Page 17. **Manuel** :
Mailman : a person who delivers mail or letters or packages
Mittens : soft coverings for the hands with just a large part and a thumb part - 4 fingers in the large part

Page 18. **Miss Morgan** : a formal name
Mistress : a woman in authority
Mandarin : a type of Chinese language
Muskrat : a large rodent with musky odor

Page 19. **Manx** - a cat with little or no tail
Mirror : a reflecting surface - usually metal with glass to see an image of the same in it
My : a word to indicate you possess something personally
Magnificent : splendid, super, excellent, very beautiful

Page 20. **Mallard** - a bird in the duck family
Mattress - a large pad of different material - foam, feathers, or air, for reclining or sleeping

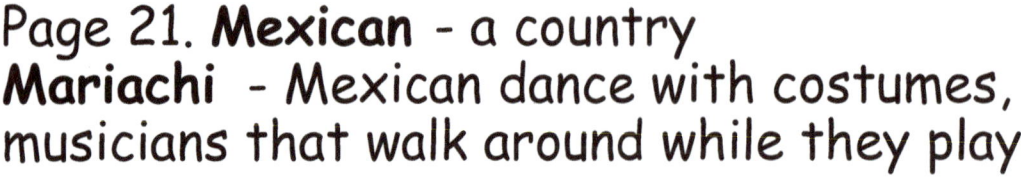

Page 21. **Mexican** - a country
Mariachi - Mexican dance with costumes, musicians that walk around while they play

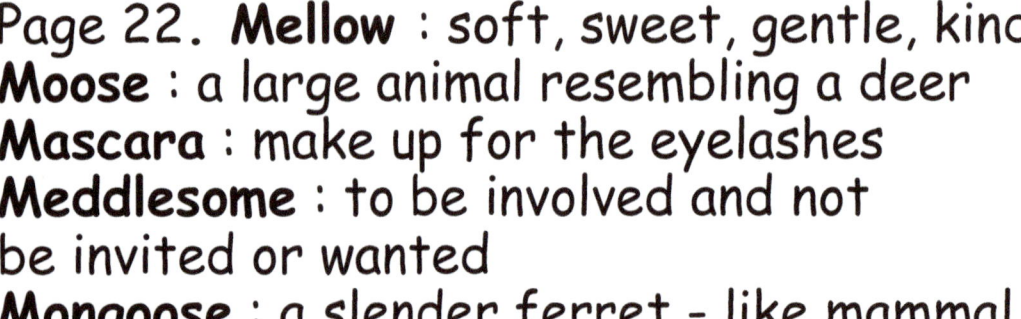

Page 22. **Mellow** : soft, sweet, gentle, kind
Moose : a large animal resembling a deer
Mascara : make up for the eyelashes
Meddlesome : to be involved and not be invited or wanted
Mongoose : a slender ferret - like mammal
mild : gentle behavior toward others or less spicy tasting
Mayonnaise : a thick whitish dressing of egg yolks, vinegar, and lemon juice

Page 23. **Mabel** :
Merengue : a ballroom dance that is where they are stiff legged and jump or hop or limp during the dance
Mule : a large animal that resembles a horse
Maracas : a musical instrument

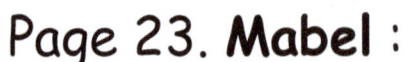

Page 24. **Magpie** : a bird
Muttering : talk in a low volume so you cannot really understand
Magenta : a color
Mosquitoes : a small winged insect with a large nose to pierce skin or flowers with

Page 25. **Morris** :
Many : a large number of
Marine : relating to the sea - come from the sea, live in the sea
Muscles : tissue composed of cells and fibers that shorten and lengthen and cause movement of body parts

Page 26. **Michelle** :
Mainly : for the most part
Mouthpiece : the part of the instrument where one will put their mouth around

Page 28. **Mrs.Marigold** : formal name
Mandolin - a musical instrument
Majestic - grand, wonderful
Mermaid - a mythical lady with the head and body of a woman and the legs of a fish like a tail of a fish

Page 29. **Married** : two people who promise to be together forever, combined
Mammoth : a large elephant-like creature that is now extinct
Mojo : ability, charming, having fun
Monstrously : in a very large manner, sometimes over able, big
Moves : change location or position from one place to another
Melodies : musical sounds that are pleasant and sweet to others

Page 30. **Mice** : furry little rodents
Music store : a place where music and musical instruments are sold

Page 31. **Mixed** : to combine things or put things together
Middle : equal distance from both sides
M : a letter

Page 32. **Many** : a large number of
More : additional, greater amount or number

Paula Curtis-Taylorson Lives in Marston Mortaine England. She is a full-time secondary school teacher of English and English Literature. She was amongst the first of the initial students to graduate from the Uk's first BA (Hons) Creative Writing Program at the University of Bedfordshire.

    Her first love is poetry and rhyme and she works hard to inspire and teach appreciation of the subject to all age groups. Many of her students have gone on to be successful writers.

www.ingramcontent.com/pod-product-compliance
Lightning Source LLC
Chambersburg PA
CBHW061105070526